FINAL REPORT: CULPEPER COUNTY [VIRGINIA] ROAD ORDERS

1763-1764

Virginia Genealogical Society
Richmond, Virginia

Published With Permission from the

Virginia Transportation Research Council
(A Cooperative Organization Sponsored Jointly by the Virginia
Department of Transportation and
the University of Virginia)

HERITAGE BOOKS
2008

HERITAGE BOOKS
AN IMPRINT OF HERITAGE BOOKS, INC.

Books, CDs, and more—Worldwide

For our listing of thousands of titles see our website
at
www.HeritageBooks.com

Published 2008 by
HERITAGE BOOKS, INC.
Publishing Division
100 Railroad Avenue #104
Westminster, Maryland 21157

International Standard Book Number: 978-0-7884-3659-8

FINAL REPORT

CULPEPER COUNTY ROAD ORDERS 1763-1764

Ann Brush Miller
Consultant
Culpeper County Historical Society

(The opinions, findings, and conclusions expressed in this report are those of the author and not necessarily those of the sponsoring agencies.)

Virginia Transportation Research Council
(A Cooperative Organization Sponsored Jointly by the Virginia
Department of Transportation and
the University of Virginia)

Charlottesville, Virginia

June 1994
Revised May 2004
VTRC 94-TAR13

HISTORIC ROADS OF VIRGINIA

Louisa County Road Orders 1742-1748, by Nathaniel Mason Pawlett. 57 pages, indexed, map.

Goochland County Road Orders 1728-1744, by Nathaniel Mason Pawlett. 120 pages, indexed, map.

Albemarle County Road Orders 1744-1748, by Nathaniel Mason Pawlett. 57 pages, indexed, map.

The Route of the Three Notch'd Road, by Nathaniel Mason Pawlett and Howard Newlon. 26 pages, illustrated, 2 maps.

An Index to Roads in the Albemarle County Surveyor Books 1744-1853, by Nathaniel Mason Pawlett, 10 pages, map.

A Brief History of the Staunton and James River Turnpike, by Douglas Young. 22 pages, illustrated, map.

Albemarle County Road Orders 1783-1816, by Nathaniel Mason Pawlett. 421 pages, indexed.

A Brief History of the Roads of Virginia 1607-1840, by Nathaniel Mason Pawlett. 41 pages

A Guide to the Preparation of County Road Histories, by Nathaniel Mason Pawlett. 26 pages, 2 maps.

Early Road Location: Key to Discovering Historic Resources? By Nathaniel Mason Pawlett and K. Edward Lay. 47 pages, illustrated, 3 maps.

Albemarle County Road Orders 1725-1816, by Nathaniel Mason Pawlett. 98 pages, illustrated, 8 maps.

"Backsights," A Bibliography, by Nathaniel Mason Pawlett. 29 pages,

Orange County Road Orders 1734-1749, by Ann Brush Miller. 323 pages, indexed, map.

Spotsylvania County Road Orders 1722-1734, by Nathaniel Mason Pawlett. 159 pages, indexed.

Brunswick County Road Orders 1732-1749, by Nathaniel Mason Pawlett. 81 pages, indexed.

Orange County Road Orders 1750-1800, by Ann Brush Miller. 394 pages, indexed, map.

Lunenburg County Road Orders 1746-1764, by Nathaniel Mason Pawlett and Tyler Jefferson Boyd, 302 pages, indexed.

Library of Congress Catalogue Card
94-060228

PREFACE

HOW THIS WORK CAME INTO BEING

by

Nathaniel Mason Pawlett
Faculty Research Historian
Virginia Transportation Research Council

The importance of the preparation of a detailed history of the early roads of each Virginian county can hardly be overstated. Most of this early road network still remains in place and in service. With subsequent, sometimes extremely subtile, changes in emphasis, and with a few additions here and there, it has over the years provided the lines along which Virginia's social, political and economic life has flowed. Indeed, the fate of the nation has at times been determined by the shape of this road network. Beyond this, road history and its supporting documents are becoming more and more relevant to a growing number of disciplines from anthropology and architectural history through environmental science, folklore, genealogy, and history to sociology.

Local historians and genealogists, perhaps the most obvious groups to which these publications are useful, have also a vested interest in seeing that more of these road histories are completed. Moreover, these are the people with the specialised knowledge of local history and genealogy so necessary to the writing of a competent road history. If in our time this massive picture puzzle whose pieces still lie before us in a heap is to be reassembled, an effort must soon be made. These present modest efforts are the pioneering ones, designed only to begin the task by attempting to sketch in broad outlines those roads laid down during the first 50 years after settlement in the area presently contained in each of Virginia's counties. That this must be done by local people, or those with a similar orientation and knowledge, should be obvious. That it must be done in this generation, before the rapidly quickening pace of urban and suburban development obliterates much of the visual evidence, is manifest. Local historians and genealogists are therefore summoned to a duty which has perhaps already been too long delayed in many areas, the collection and publication of their road orders and the research and writing of histories of their early county roads. Culpeper County Road Orders 1763-1764 is an early effort in this direction by a local group. It is fourth in the series on roads in early Spotsylvania County and its progeny counties which began with Spotsylvania County Road Orders 1722-1734, published by the Virginia Transportation Research Council. This volume was followed by Orange County Road Orders 1734-1749 and Orange County Road Orders 1750-1800, published in cooperation with the Orange County Historical Society.

The Culpeper County Historical Society, under the leadership of their president, William H. Martin, commissioned the present volume as a continuation of this series. This volume is rendered doubly significant by the fact that virtually all of the pre-Revolutionary court records for Culpeper County were destroyed during the Civil War. The road orders in this volume provide the only extant evidence for transportation-related records for Culpeper County during this period. In the face of the destruction of many of the original records, the transcription and collection of the surviving road orders in this volume will enable the most accurate research possible into the early road history of Culpeper County.

FINAL REPORT

CULPEPER COUNTY ROAD ORDERS 1763-1764

by

Ann Brush Miller
Consultant
Culpeper County Historical Society

INTRODUCTION

The roads are under the government of the county courts, subject to be controuled by the general court. They order new roads to be opened whenever they think them necessary. The inhabitants of the county are by them laid off into precincts, to each of which they allot a convenient portion of the public roads to be kept in repair. Such bridges as may be built without the assistance of artificers, they are to be built. If the stream be such as to require a bridge of regular workmanship, the court employs workmen to build it, at the expense of the whole county. If it be too great for the county, application is made to the general assembly, who authorize individuals to build it, and to take a fixed toll from all passengers, or give sanction to such other proposition as to them appears reasonable.

Thomas Jefferson, *Notes on the State of Virginia*, 1781

The establishment and maintenance of public roads was one of the most important functions of the County Court during the colonial period in Virginia. Each road was opened and maintained by an Overseer of Highways appointed by the Gentlemen Justices yearly. He was usually assigned all the "Labouring Male Titheables" living on or near the road for this purpose. These individuals then furnished all their own tools, wagons, and teams and were required to labour for six days each year on the roads.

Major projects, such as bridges over rivers, demanding considerable expenditures were executed by Commissioners appointed by the Court to select the site and to contract with workmen for the construction. Where bridges connected two counties, a commission was appointed by each and they cooperated in executing the work.

At its creation from Orange County in 1749, Culpeper County comprised most of the region between the Rapidan and Rappahannock rivers: the present counties of Culpeper, Madison and Rappahannock. From this territory would be cut the counties of Madison (created in 1793) and Rappahannock (1833), leaving the remainder of Culpeper County at its present boundaries.

The Culpeper Court Minute Books for most of the 18th century were destroyed during the Civil War. The partial Minute Book for the years 1763-1764 is the only Court Minute Book to survive for the period when the territory of Culpeper County was at its largest extent. The road orders contained within this volume constitute the sole transportation-related court orders surviving for Culpeper County during this period.

Note: As originally published in paper format, this volume included maps showing the evolution of the county. Maps are not included in the revised/electronic version due to legibility and file size considerations. Instead, a verbal description is provided.

Prior to 1720, the area that is now Culpeper County was part of the far western reaches of Essex County. In 1720, the present territory of Culpeper County was included within newly-formed Spotsylvania County, which included the present counties of Spotsylvania, Orange, Greene, Culpeper, Madison, and Rappahannock east of the Blue Ridge Mountains, and a portion of the Shenandoah Valley as far west as the Shenandoah River.

In 1734, Orange County was created from Spotsylvania County. A giant county at its formation, Orange included the present-day counties of Orange, Greene, Culpeper, Madison, and Rappahannock east of the Blue Ridge Mountains, as well as the territory west of the mountains extending, at least nominally, to the Mississippi River.

In 1749, the northern portion of Orange County lying east of the Blue Ridge and north of the Rapidan River was cut off as Culpeper County. As created from Orange County, Culpeper County contained the present counties of Culpeper, Madison and Rappahannock. Madison County was created in 1793, and Rappahannock County in 1833, leaving Culpeper County at its present boundaries.

MINUTE BOOK OF CULPEPER COUNTY 1763-1764

(NOTE: only pages 271 through 477 survive; many are mutilated)

[March?] 1763, p. 271
Ordered That Richard Gaines be appointed Surveyor of Hig[hways?--page torn] from the Hazel River to Thorntons Pass in the room of J[torn] McDaniel and that the Hands appointed on the said Road [torn] him and Obey his Direction in Clearing & keeping the same.

[March?] 1763, p. 271
On the Petition of Michael Smith and Others for a Convenient [torn] from Tevault Christlers to the Dutch Church through the Plantation [torn] Harrensparger's decd. Ordered That James Barbour Gent, Ell[iott?--page torn] Bohannon, William Walker and Ephraim Rucker or any [torn] of them being first sworn before a Justice of the Peace for this County [torn] View & report to the Court the Conveniency it may be to the Pet[itioners?--page torn] and also the Damage [illegible] the Lands of the said [torn] any other Person whatsoever.

[March?] 1763, p. 271
On the Motion of William Stanton in behalf of himself & others [torn] from Joseph Eddin's into the old road Ordered that Jeremiah [rest of entry illegible]

17 March 1763, p. 274
Ordered that William Pritchett be Appointed Surveyor of the Roads from his House & from Richard Rennolds's to the Road near the Widow Johnston's in the room of William Hansford and that the Hands Appointed on the said Roads do Attend him and Obey his Directions in Clearing & keeping the same in Lawful Repair.

17 March 1763, p. 276
On the Motion of George Kinnaird he has Leave to keep an Ordinary at the fork of Finleson's Road below the Church giving Bond & Security as the Law Directs.

17 March 1763, p. 277
[most of entry torn] keeping the same in lawful repair.

17 March 1763, p. 277
On the Petition of Lewis Davis Yancey for leave to turn the Road at [his?--page torn] lower Plantation to the other side of his Line Ordered That Capt. Francis Slaughter, Thomas Covington, William Slaughter, & John Faver or any three of them being first sworn before a Justice of the Peace for this County do View the same and report to the Court the Conveiency and Inconveniency it may be to the Public the Petitioner or any other Person.

17 March 1763, p. 277
On the Motion of John Flint It is Ordered that he be exempted from the Payment of his County Levy for the future.

17 March 1763, p. 278
A View and report on the Motion of William Stanton & others for a Road from Joseph Eddins's Plantation into the old Road, was this Day returned Ordered that the Petitioners have Leave to Clear the same agreeable to the said View & report.

18 March 1763, p. 279
The Petition of Joseph Eddins for a Road from his House into the Main Road no return being made it is Ordered to be Dismissed.

[Fragmentary page bound between pages 289 and 290; date mutilated: _____,___1763]

On the Motion of Courtney Norman to turn [torn--the road that?] leads to Chesters at his Plantation whereupon It is Ordered [torn] Hickman, Edwin Hickman, Moredock McKinzie, & John [torn] view the same and report to the Court the Conveniency & Inconveniency it may to the Public, the Petitioner or any other [torn].

21 April 1763, p. 305
Ordered That Gerrard Banks be Appointed Surveyor of the Road from the Point of the Fork to the new Frederickburgh Road in the room of Simon Miller and that the Hands Appointed on the said do Attend him & Obey his Direction in Clearing & keeping the same in Lawfull Repair.

21 April 1763, p. 306
On the Motion of Michael Sloane by his Attorney he has Leave to keep an Ordinary at his House in this County Giving Bond & Security According to Law.

21 April 1763, p. 306
A View and report on the Petition of Lewis Davis Yancey to turn the Road on the Line of his Land at his Lower Plantation was this Day returned Ordered he have Leave to turn the same agreeable to the said View & report Clearing the same According to Law.

21 April 1763, p. 306
A View & report on the Petition of Charles Kavanaugh to turn the Road at his Plantation this Day the Viewers made their report Ordered that they have Leave to Clear the same Agreeable to the said View & report According to Law.

21 April 1763, p. 306
On the Motion of Thomas Pratt to be removed from Thorntons Road to the road leading from the same to Bradleys Mill Ordered that the said Thomas Pratt James Shearer & John Weekley do work on the last Mentioned Road under Benjamin Thomas Overseer.

21 April 1763, p. 308
On the Motion of Joseph James his Ordinary Licence is renewed giving Bond & Security According to Law.

21 April 1763, p. 308
On the Motion of James Finnie for Leave to turn the Road at his Plantation Ordered That Elliott Bohannon, William Booton, William Rice & William Walker or any three of them being first sworn before a Justice of the Peace for this County do View the same & report to the Court the Conveniency & Inconveniency it may be to the Petitioner the Public or any other Person.

21 April 1763, p. 309
On the Motion of Nathaniel Pendleton Gent his Ordinary Licence is renewed giving Bond & Security according to Law.

21 April 1763, p. 310
On the Motion of John Mcgannan Leave is given him to keep an Ordinary at his House in this County giving Bond & security According to Law.

22 April 1763, p. 316
The View and report for a road from Cornelius Mitchell's to the County line leading towards Fauquier Courthouse is Continued for the Court to consider thereof.

22 April 1763, p. 319
Ordered That John Rawson be appointed Surveyor of the Roads whereof Archibald Gillison was late Overseer and that the Hands Appointed on the said Roads do Attend him & Obey his Direction in Clearing & keeping the same in Lawful repair.

22 April 1763, p. 319
On Courtney Normans Petition to turn the road at his Plantation this Day the Viewers made their report whereupon he has Leave to turn the same agreeable thereto Clearing it According to Law.

19 May 1763, p. 322
Upon the Petition of William Robertson & others to have their Antient Rowling Way & Church Way Established Ordered that James Spilman, Christopher Hutchins, John Barbee & John Read or any three of them being first sworn before a Justice of the Peace for this County [torn] the sayd Ways & Make [torn] thereof to the next Court.

19 May 1763, p. 323
On the Petition of Michael Smith and others for a Convenient Way Road from Tevalt Chrislers to the Dutch Church through the Plantation of Joseph Harrensparger decd. the Viewers this Day made their Report whereupon they have Leave to Clear the same in November next agreeable to the said View & report.

19 May 1763, p. 323
On the motion of John Corbin his Ordinary Licence is renewed giving Bond & Security According to Law.

19 May 1763, p. 323
[Grand Jury Presentments]
"We do likewise Present the Overseer of the Road from the fork of the road below stony Hill to Kinnaird's Ordinary in St. Marks Parish within Six months last past"

19 May 1763, p. 324
[Grand Jury Presentments]
"We present the Overseer of the Road that [torn] the Road above Alexander McQueen's and Leads to [torn] part in Saint Marks Parish & Part in Brumfield within Six Months last past"

19 May 1763, p. 327
On the Petition of James Finnie for leave to turn the Road at his Plantation, the Viewers this Day made their Report which was Objected to by William Kirtley Gent and the Parties being fully heard it is Ordered That the new Way be continued till the next fall and that then the old Way be Established.

19 May 1763, p. 327
On the Motion of Christopher Crigler It is Ordered That James Shurley be appointed Surveyor of the Road from the Robinson River to a Pine on Muddy Run in his room and that the Hands Appinted on the said Road do Attend him & Obed his Direction in Clearing & keeping the same in Lawful repair

19 May 1763, p. 330
Ordered that John Jett be appointed Surveyor of the Road from Grinnals's Foard to Mill run in the room of Dickie Latham and that the Hands Appointed on the said Roads do Attend him & Obey his Direction in Clearing & keeping the same in Lawful repair.

21 May 1763 (?) [loose page inserted between p. 358 and 359]
[torn]..[from?] the Bowling to Cornelius Mitchell's in the room of [torn] and that the Hands appointed on the said Road do Attend him [torn]his Direction in Clearing and keeping the same in Lawful re[pair]

21 May 1763, p. 363
Ordered That James Pendleton be appointed Surveyor of the Roads whereof Henry Pendleton Gent was late Overseer and that the Hands Appointed on the said Roads do Attend him & Obey his direction in Clearing & keeping the same in lawfull Repair

21 May 1763, p. 364
Ordered that the Hands appointed on the Road from the Courthouse to Thorntons Road
under John Reynolds Overseer be Exempted from working on all other Roads

16 June 1763, p. 365
On the Motion of Frederick Zimmerman his Ordinary Licence is renewed his giving
Bond & Security According to Law

16 June 1763, p. 366
On the Petition of Henry Netherton & others to have the Antient Road Established at
Courtney Norman's Plantation Alledging that the new Way turned by order of this Court
is Impassible for Waggons, Whereupon It is Ordered that William Eastham Gent,
William Russell, John Frogg & James Kennerley or any three of them first sworn before
a Justice of the Peace for the County aforesaid do View as well the New Way as the Old
Road and report to the Court the Conveniency & Inconveniency it may be to the Public,
Courtney Norman or any other Person.

16 June 1763, p. 366
Upon the Petition of William Robertson & others to have their antient Rowling Way &
Church Way Eastablished This Day the Viewers made their Report whereon It is Ordered
that they have Leave to Clear the said Ways and that they be Established for the future
agreeable to the said View & report

16 June 1763, p. 366
Ordered that Cornelius Mitchell be appointed Surveyor of the Road leading to Chesters
Gap in the same precinct as Thomas Corbin was late Overseer & that the Gang of Hands
appointed on the said Road do Attend him & Obey his Direction in Clearing and keeping
the same in Lawfull repair

16 June 1763, p. 368
On the Petition of John Leer junr Suggesting that the Rowling Way & Church way
Petitioned for by Wm. Robertson & others According to View & report made thereon
will be of great prejudice to him & praying there may be a review thereof, whereupon It
is Ordered That Christopher Hoomes, John Green, John Read & George Parsons or any
three of them being first sworn before a Justice of the Peace for this County do View a
Way from Robert Hoppers into the Road that leads to the Church and report to the Court
the Conveniency & Inconveniency it may be to Public, the Petitioner, or any other
Person.

16 June 1763, p. 369
Ordered that Anthony Head be appointed Surveyor of the road from Pophams Run to Ashleys Foard and that the Hands Appointed on the said Road do Attend him & obey his Direction in Clearing & keeping the same in lawfull Repair

16 June 1763, p. 369
Ordered that Thomas Chelton be appointed Surveyor of the Road from the Hazel River to F.T. in the room of Timothy Sisk and that the Hands appointed on the said Road do Attend him & Obey his Direction in Clearing & keeping the same in Lawfull repair

21 July 1763, p. 375
Ordered That John Humphreys be Appointed Surveyor of the Road from Nick's Gallows to Scotts Bridge & tht Henry Pendleton Gent. do Settle & Divide the Hands between him & Cornelius Mitchell the former Overseer and that the said Humphreys with the Hands so Allotted him do Clear & keep the same in Lawfull repair

22 July 1763, p. 384
Ordered That Thomas Slaughter, William Green & Benjamin Roberts Gent. or any two of them do View the Bridge Built over Brookes's Run and report to the Court whether the same is performed according to Agreement

22 July 1763, p. 386
On the Petition of Henry Netherton & others to have the Antient Way Established as the road at Courtney Normans Plantation the former Order not being Complied with it is Ordered that John Frogg, James Kennerley, John Roberts & Robert Detherage or any three of them being first Sworn before a Justice of the Peace for this County do View as well the new Way as the old Road & report to the Court the Conveniency, Inconveniency it may be to the Public the said Courtney Norman or any othe Person

23 July 1763, p. 395
The Petition of John Leer junr. for a review of a Road is Continued for the Viewers to make their Report till the next Court

8 August 1763, p. 408
The View and report on the Petition of John Leer for a review of the Church Way from Hoppers to the Church Way &c This Day the Viewers made their report Ordered that the way last Viewed be Established as the Church Way

20 August 1763, p. 433
The Petition of Henry Netherton & others to establish the Old way of the Road at Courtney Normans Plantation is Continued for the Viewers to make their Report at the next Court

15 September 1763, p. 448
On the Motion of John Carpenter junr. Nicholas Yeager, Nicholas Smith, Matthias Smith Christopher Barlor & Jacob Barlor to be Added to the Gang on the Road whereof John Yeager is Overseer Ordered that they do Attend the said Yeager & Obey his Direction in Clearing the keeping the said Road in Lawfull repair and that they be Exempted all other Roads

15 December 1763, p. 462
On the Motion of Robert Green Gent. his Ordinary Licence is renewed giving Bond & Security According to Law

15 December 1763, p. 462
[County Levy]

	lb Tob°.
To John Spotswood Esqr. decd. Estate for keeping Germa. Ferry	3000
To Robert Leavell for setting up a Post of Directions	50
To John Thomas for a post of Direction P Accot	50
To pay Ambrose Camp L 5. for services done the County & to Pay Peter Taliaferro for building a Bridge over Brookes Run to be	3500

15 December 1763, p. 463
On the Motion of Frances Browning for a Rolling Road through the Land of John Cooper, this Day the Viewers made their Report whereupon the Petitioner

prayed to have a review of the same, Ordered that the same Viewers (to wit) William Johnston Junr, William Duncan, John Roberts, & Reuben Slaughter or any three being first Sworn before a Justice of the Peace for this County do View the several ways proposed from her Plantation into the Road and make report of the Conveniences & Inconveniences it may be to the Petitioner the said Cooper or any other Person to the next Court

15 December 1763, p. 464
Ordered That Nathaniel Pendleton Gent do Acquaint Bernard Moore Esqr. of John Spotswood Esqr. decd. that unless there be better Attendance given and better Cannoes kept for the Transportation of Tobacco &c at Germanna ferry for the future that this Court will withdraw the salary that they Annually have Allowed: and pursue such Steps as by Law pointed out in Such Cases

19 January 1764, p. 467
On the motion of James Slaughter Gent. for a Road from the Schoolhouse by Archibald Gillisons to his Mill Ordered That Christopher Hutchins, John Barbee, James Spilman, & Archibald Gillison do View the same being first sworn before a Justice of the Peace for this County and make return thereof to the next Court

19 January 1764, p. 467
On the Motion of Henry Field Gent for a Road from Thorntons Road a little below Madam Thornton's Quarter to the North branch of the Hazel River commonly called the Great Wilderness Ordered that Timothy Sisk, James White, John Grayson, & Richard Gaines or any three of them being first sworn before a Justice of the Peace for this County do View and Lay off the most Convenient way for Carrying the same and make report thereof to the next Court

19 January 1764, p. 467
On the Motion of Frances Browning for a Rolling Road from her Plantation through the Land of John Cooper and for a review thereof which is Continued till the next Court

____ February 1764, p. 472 (470?)
On the Motion of James Barbour junr Gent. for leave to turn the Road from or near the White Oak Run through an old Field belonging to Adam Gaar to his Rolling Road and thence with the same to the Main Road Ordered That James Rucker, Ephraim Rucker Elliott Bohannon & William Walker or any three of them being first sworn before a Justice of the Peace for the said County do View the same & make return thereof to the next Court

____ February 1764, p. 472 (470?)
The View and report on the Motion of James Slaughter Gent for a Road to issue out of the Road that Leads from Freeman's to Grinnals' Foard near the Schoolhouse by Gillisons to his Mill, was this Day returned whereupon It is Ordered that John Jett and Frederick Fishback with their Gang of Hands under them do Clear & Open the same According to the said View & report

--- No more road order entries in the surviving Minute Book for 1763-1764 ---

Index

This index is arranged by subject: Personal Names; Bridges; County Property and Establishments; Chapels, Churches, Parishes and Glebes; Ferries; Fords; Houses, Lands, Plantations and Quarters; Mills; Mountains, Gaps and Passes; Neighborhoods, Towns and Landmarks; Ordinaries and Ordinary Licenses; Water Features; Roads

Pendleton, Henry, Gent., 9, 11
    James, 9
    Nathaniel, Gent., 7, 13
Popham, 10
Pratt, Thomas, 7
Pritchett, William, 5
Rawson, John, 8
Read, John, 8, 10
Rennolds, Richard, 5
Reynolds, John, 9
Rice, William, 7
Roberts, Benjamin, Gent., 11
    John, 11, 12
Robertson, William, 8, 10(2)
Rucker, Ephraim, 5, 13
    James, 13
Russell, William, 10
Scott, 11
Shearer, James, 7
Shurley, James, 9
Sisk, Timothy, 11, 13
Slaughter, Capt. Francis, 6
    James, Gent., 13(2)
    Reuben, 12
    Thomas, 11
    William, 6
Sloane, Michael, 6
Smith, Michael, 5, 8
    Nicholas, 12
Spilman, James, 13
Spotswood, John, Esqr., dec., 12, 13
Stanton, William, 5, 6
Taliaferro, Peter, 12
Thomas, Benjamin, 7
    John, 12
Thornton, 5, 7, 9, 13
Thornton, Madam, 13
Walker, William, 5, 7, 13
Weekley, John, 7
White, James, 13
Yancey, Lewis Davis, 6, 7
Yeager, John, 12
    Nicholas, 12
Zimmerman, Frederick, 10

Bridges
bridge over Brookes's Run, 11, 12
Scott's bridge, 11

County Property and Establishments
County Levy, 6, 12
County line (with Fauquier County), 8
the [Culpeper County] Courthouse, 9
Fauquier Courthouse, 8

see also **Courthouse Roads**

Chapels, Churches, Parishes and Glebes
the Church, 5, 10
the Dutch Church, 5, 8
Brumfield Parish, 9
St. Mark's Parish, 8, 9

see also **Church roads**

Ferries
Germanna ferry, 12, 13

Fords
Ashley's, 10
Grinnal's, 9, 13

Houses, Lands, Plantations and Quarters
Frances Browning's plantation, 13
Chester's, 6
Tevault Christler's, 5, 8
John Cooper's land, 12, 13
Joseph Eddin's house/plantation, 5, 6(2)
James Finnie's plantation, 7, 9
Freeman's, 13
Adam Gaar's old field, 13
Archibald Gillison's, 13(2)
Joseph Harrensparger, dec's
    Plantation, 5, 8
Robert Hopper's, 10, 11
Widow Johnston's, 5
Charles Kavanaugh's plantation, 7
John McGannan's house, 7
Alexander McQueen's, 9

Cornelius Mitchell's, 9
Courtney Norman's plantation, 6, 8, 10, 11, 12
William Pritchett's house, 5
Richard Rennolds's, 5
Michael Sloane's house, 6
Madam Thornton's quarter, 13
Lewis Davis Yancy's lower plantation, 6, 7

Popham's Run, 10
Robinson River, 9
White Oak Run, 13

Mills
Bradley's, 7
Archibald Gillison's, 13(2)

Mountains, Gaps and Passes
Chester's Gap, 10
Stony Hill, 8
Thornton's Pass, 5

Neighborhoods, Towns and Landmarks
the Bowling, 9
Fredericksburg, 6
F.T., 11
Germanna, 12, 13
Nick's Gallows, 11
the Great Wilderness, 13
the Schoolhouse by Archibald Gillison's, 13(2)

Ordinaries and Ordinary Licenses
Corbin, John, 8
Robert Green, Gent., 12
Joseph James, 7
George Kinnaird/Kinnaird's ordinary, 5, 8
John McGannan, 7
Nathaniel Pendleton, 7
Michael Sloane, 6

Water Features
Brookes's Run, 11, 12
Hazel River, 5, 11, 13
Muddy Run, 9
Mill Run, 9
Point of the fork, 6

Roads

A

road from Popham's Run to <u>Ashley's</u> ford, 10

B

road from the <u>Bowling</u> to Cornelius Mitchell's, 9

rolling road from Frances <u>Browning's</u> plantation through John Cooper's land, 12, 13

C

road from Courtney Norman's plantation to <u>Chester's</u>, 6, 8

road to <u>Chester's</u> Gap, 10

road from Tevault <u>Christler's</u> to the Dutch Church through the plantation of Joseph Harrensparger, dec., 5, 8

road from Tevault Christler's to the <u>Dutch Church</u> through the plantation of Joseph Harrensparger, dec., 5, 8

forks of Finleson's Road below the <u>Church</u>, 5

road from Robert Hopper's into the road to the <u>Church,</u> 10, 11(2)

road by William Robertson's and others' lands (their ancient rolling way and <u>church</u> way), 8, 10(2)

rolling road from Frances Browning's plantation through John <u>Cooper's</u> land, 12, 13

road from Cornelius Mitchell's to the <u>County line</u> leading towards Fauquier Courthouse, 8

road from the <u>Courthouse</u> to Thornton's road, 9

E

road from Joseph <u>Eddin's</u> into the old road, 5, 6

road from Joseph <u>Eddins's</u> into the main road, 6

F

road from Cornelius Mitchell's to the County line leading towards <u>Fauquier</u> Courthouse, 8

road from the point of the fork to the new <u>Fredericksburgh</u> Road, 6

forks of <u>Finleson's</u> Road below the Church, 5

road at James <u>Finnie's</u> plantation, 7, 9

road from <u>Freeman's</u> to Grinnal's ford, 13

road from Hazel River to <u>F.T.</u>, 11

G

road turning out from the main road near White Oak Run, thence through an old field of Adam <u>Gaar's</u> to his rolling road, and with the rolling road to the main road, 13

road from the schoolhouse by Archibald <u>Gillisons</u> to his mill (road leading out of the road from Freeman's to Grinnal's ford near the Schoolhouse, thence by Archibald <u>Gillison's</u> to his mill), 13(2)

road from <u>Grinnal's</u> ford to Mill Run, 9

road from the schoolhouse by Archibald Gillisons to his mill (road leading out of the road from Freeman's to <u>Grinnal's</u> ford near the Schoolhouse, thence by Archibald Gillison's to his mill), 13(2)

H

road from Tevault Christler's to the Dutch Church through the plantation of Joseph <u>Harrensparger</u>, dec., 5, 8

road from <u>Hazel River</u> to F.T., 11

road from the <u>Hazel River</u> to Thornton's Pass, 5

road from Thornton's road below Madam Thornton's quarter to the north branch of the <u>Hazel River</u>, commonly called the Great Wilderness, 13

road from Robert <u>Hopper's</u> into the road to the Church, 10, 11(2)

J

road from William Pritchett's house and Richard Rennold's to the road near the Widow <u>Johnston's</u>, 5

K

road at Charles Kavanaugh's plantation, 7

road from the fork of the road below Stony Hill to Kinnaird's Ordinary, 8

M

road above Alexander McQueen's (part in St. Mark's Parish and part in Brumfield Parish), 9

road from Grinnal's ford to Mill Run, 9

road from Cornelius Mitchell's to the County line leading towards Fauquier Courthouse, 8

road from the Bowling to Cornelius Mitchell's, 9

road from the Robinson River to Muddy Run, 9

N

road from Nick's Gallows to Scott's bridge, 11

road from Courtney Norman's plantation to Chester's, 6, 8

old road at Courtney Norman's plantation, 10, 11, 12

P

road above Alexander McQueen's (part in St. Mark's Parish and part in Brumfield Parish), 9

road from Popham's Run to Ashley's ford, 10

road from William Pritchett's house and Richard Rennold's to the road near the Widow Johnston's, 5

R

road from William Pritchett's house and Richard Rennold's to the road near the Widow Johnston's, 5

road by William Robertson's and others' lands (their ancient rolling way and church way), 8, 10(2) road from the <u>Robinson River</u> to Muddy Run, 9

S

road from Nick's Gallows to <u>Scott's</u> bridge, 11

road from the <u>Schoolhouse</u> by Archibald Gillisons to his mill (road leading out of the road from Freeman's to Grinnal's ford near the <u>Schoolhouse</u>, thence by Archibald Gillison's to his mill), 13(2)

road from the fork of the road below <u>Stony Hill</u> to Kinnaird's Ordinary, 8

T

Road from the Hazel River to <u>Thornton's</u> Pass, 5

<u>Thornton's</u> road, 7, 9, 13

road from <u>Thornton's</u> road to Bradley's mill, 7

road from the Courthouse to <u>Thornton's</u> road, 9

road from <u>Thornton's</u> road below Madam <u>Thornton's</u> quarter to the north branch of the Hazel River, commonly called the Great Wilderness, 13

W

road turning out from the main road near <u>White Oak Run</u>, thence through an old field of Adam Gaar's to his rolling road, and with the rolling road to the main road, 13

road from Thornton's road below Madam Thornton's quarter to the north branch of the Hazel River, commonly called the Great <u>Wilderness</u>, 13

Y

road at Lewis Davis <u>Yancy's</u> lower plantation, 6, 7

www.ingramcontent.com/pod-product-compliance
Lightning Source LLC
LaVergne TN
LVHW061342060426
835511LV00014B/2066